DEBATING THE ISSUES

Vaccines

Patricia Hutchison

Published by AV² by Weigl
350 5th Avenue, 59th Floor New York, NY 10118
Website: www.av2books.com

Library of Congress Cataloging-in-Publication Data

Names: Hutchison, Patricia, author.
Title: Vaccines / Patricia Hutchison.
Other titles: Debate about vaccines
Description: New York, NY : AV2 by Weigl, [2019] | Series: Debating the issues | Audience: Grade 7 to 8. | Revison of: The debate about vaccines. 2018. | Includes index.
Identifiers: LCCN 2018053450 (print) | LCCN 2018054166 (ebook) | ISBN 9781489696229 (Multi User Ebook) | ISBN 9781489696236 (Single User Ebook) | ISBN 9781489696205 (hardcover : alk. paper) | ISBN 9781489696212 (softcover : alk. paper)
Subjects: LCSH: Vaccines--Juvenile literature. | Vaccination--Juvenile literature. | Vaccination--Public opinion--Juvenile literature.
Classification: LCC RA638 (ebook) | LCC RA638 .H88 2019 (print) | DDC 615.3/72--dc23
LC record available at https://lccn.loc.gov/2018053450

Printed in the United States of America in Brainerd, Minnesota
1 2 3 4 5 6 7 8 9 0 22 21 20 19 18

122018
112318

First published by North Star in 2018

Project Coordinator: Priyanka Das Designer: Ana María Vidal

Every reasonable effort has been made to trace ownership and to obtain permission to reprint copyright material. The publishers would be pleased to have any errors or omissions brought to their attention so that they may be corrected in subsequent printings.

Weigl acknowledges Getty Images, iStock, Shutterstock, and Alamy as its primary image suppliers for this title.

Vaccines

Contents

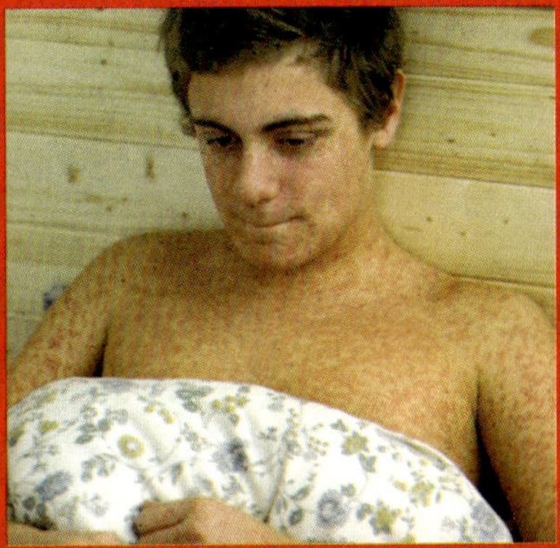

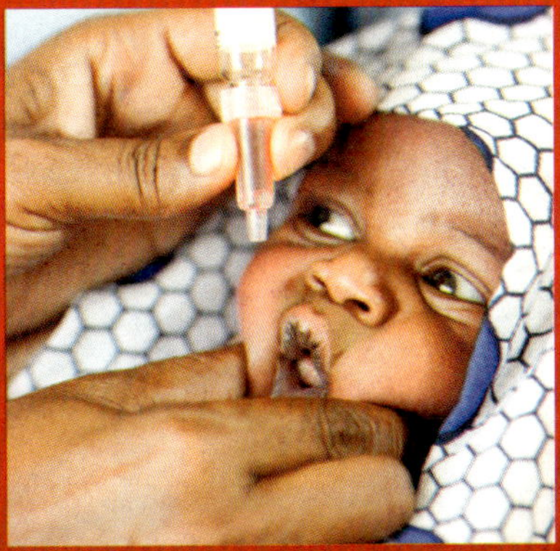

Many vaccines are administered as shots.

Understanding Vaccines

Vaccines are designed to prevent people from getting sick. When germs enter a person's body, they multiply and attack healthy cells. The body uses three kinds of white blood cells to fight back. They are macrophages, B-lymphocytes, and T-lymphocytes.

Macrophages remove germs from the bloodstream. When a disease enters the body, macrophages swoop in and gobble up germs. But dangerous **antigens** are left behind.

Lymphocytes help fight back. The body has two kinds of these specialized blood cells. B-lymphocytes produce **antibodies**. Antibodies destroy the antigens and prevent them from attacking healthy cells. Meanwhile, T-lymphocytes invade cells that have already been infected. A few T-lymphocytes stay around even after the germs are gone. If the same kind of germ invades again, the T-lymphocytes remember it. They fight the infection before the person even feels sick. This is known as immunity.

Vaccines imitate infections. Antigens in the vaccine cause the white blood cells to respond just like they would to an infection. T-lymphocytes are left behind to fight the same germs in the future. After a few doses of a vaccine, most people are immune to the disease.

Scientists produce many kinds of vaccines. Live vaccines contain a weakened form of a virus or bacteria. The weakened germs cannot reproduce easily. They will not make a person sick. Scientists also make inactivated vaccines. The germs in these vaccines are killed with heat or chemicals. For this reason, inactivated vaccines are easier to store and handle.

How a Vaccine Works

Each vaccine helps the body learn how to fight a specific disease. Vaccines train the **immune system** to respond aggressively to infections.

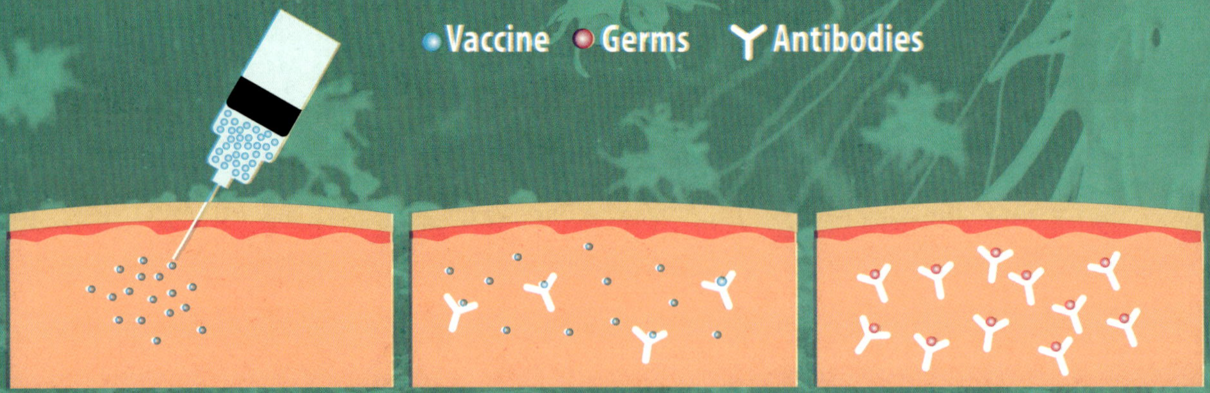

Dead or weakened germs in the vaccine enter a person's body.

The body responds to the vaccine as it would to an infection.

Antibodies remain in the body to fight the same germs in the future.

Timeline

429 BC

Thucydides, a Greek historian, notices that people who survive the deadly Plague of Athens do not become infected again.

1796 AD

English surgeon Edward Jenner uses cowpox, a mild disease, to vaccinate a boy against smallpox. The modern field of vaccination begins.

1885

The rabies vaccine is developed by French scientists Louis Pasteur and Émile Roux.

1977

After a series of global vaccinations, the last known case of smallpox occurs in Somalia. On May 8, 1980, the **World Health Organization (WHO)** declares that smallpox has been eradicated from the world.

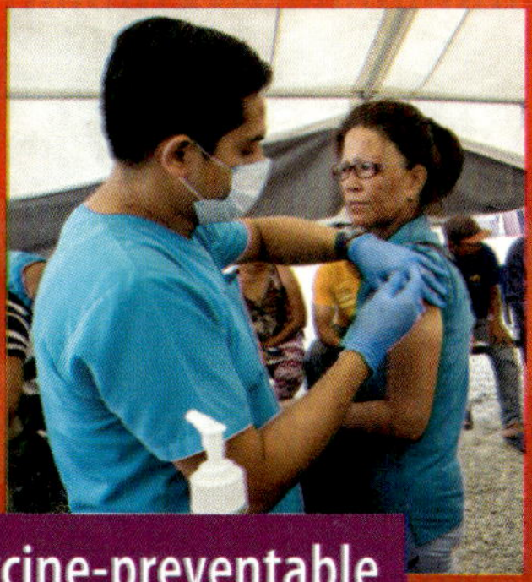

1994

Polio is reported to be completely eliminated in North and South America.

2017

There is a severe outbreak of measles, a vaccine-preventable disease, in Venezuela. It lasts for more than a year, and the Americas risk losing their official measles-free status.

PRO

Some vaccines are for serious diseases, while others are for common illnesses such as the flu.

Vaccines Prevent Deadly Diseases

Vaccines prevent illnesses that are dangerous or even deadly. For instance, smallpox killed nearly 300 million people in the 1900s. But through the years, millions of people received the smallpox vaccine. Fewer people got the disease. By 1980, smallpox had disappeared. Measles, mumps, tetanus, and polio were once common diseases, too. But because of vaccines, these illnesses are rare in most countries.

Without vaccination, 90 percent of people exposed to the measles virus will be infected.

The measles virus causes a sore throat, a fever, and a rash. It can have serious **complications**, too. These include **pneumonia** and blindness. Measles can also cause swelling of the brain or even death.

Did You Know?

Vaccines against measles, mumps, tetanus, and polio save more than two million lives each year.

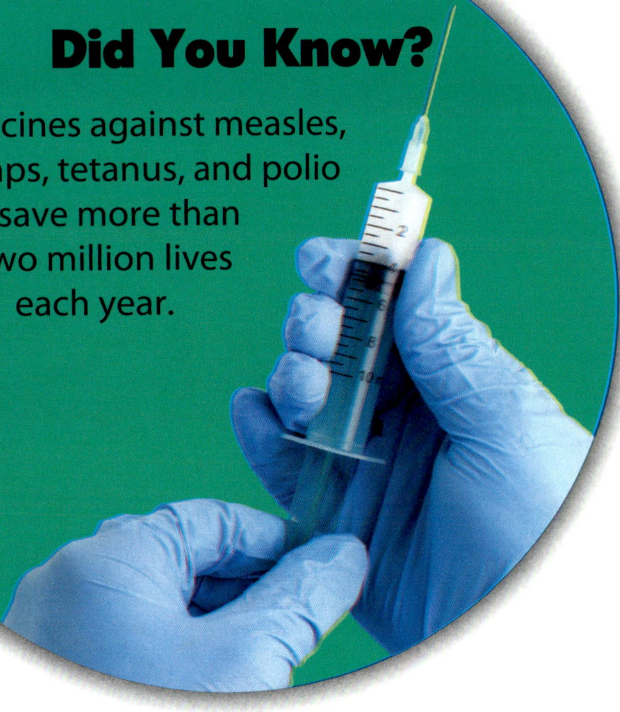

The measles vaccine was introduced in 1963. Before the vaccine, approximately four million people in the United States got measles each year. By 2004, there were only 37 cases of measles. Measles vaccines had saved more than 20 million lives worldwide by 2015.

In 2015, **15 people** across the world died from measles **every hour**.

Measles is very **infectious**. When a person with measles leaves a room, the **virus** can remain in the air for **2 hours**.

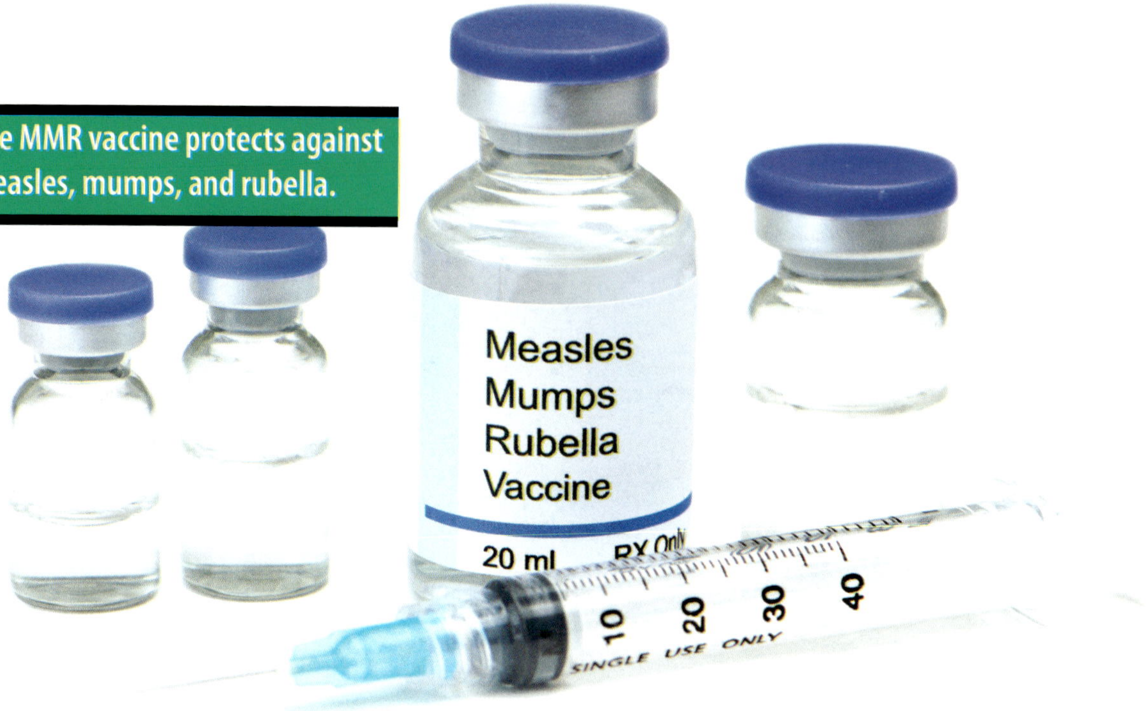

The MMR vaccine protects against measles, mumps, and rubella.

Mumps is another viral infection. People with mumps have swollen glands under their ears. Mumps can cause the **membranes** that surround the spinal cord to swell. Some people become deaf or even die as a result.

Mumps spreads easily. More than 200,000 people got the disease in 1964. A live vaccine was created in 1967. Before this vaccine, more than 150,000 people got mumps each year. Now there are fewer than 3,000 cases of mumps most years.

Tetanus is caused by bacteria. The bacteria produce a toxin that attacks the person's **nervous system**. The person's neck and jaw muscles tighten. The spasms travel to other muscles in the body, too. Soon the person cannot move at all. Most people who get tetanus die from the disease.

In the early 1940s, approximately 500 to 600 people in the United States got tetanus each year. A tetanus vaccine was introduced in the late 1940s. The number of people who get tetanus has gone down steadily since then. Between 1995 and 2015, there were fewer than 50 cases of tetanus reported each year in the United States.

Polio can spread quickly. In many people, the virus passes out of the body without making them sick. But these people can still infect others. In some cases, the polio virus attacks a person's nervous system. Less than 1 percent of people develop a high fever. Their limbs become stiff. Most recover completely. But some become **paralyzed**. They may have a disability for the rest of their lives.

A scientist invented a polio vaccine in 1953. Since then, millions of people around the world have received the vaccine. In 1988, polio caused 350,000 people around the world to become paralyzed. By 2016, fewer than 40 cases were reported.

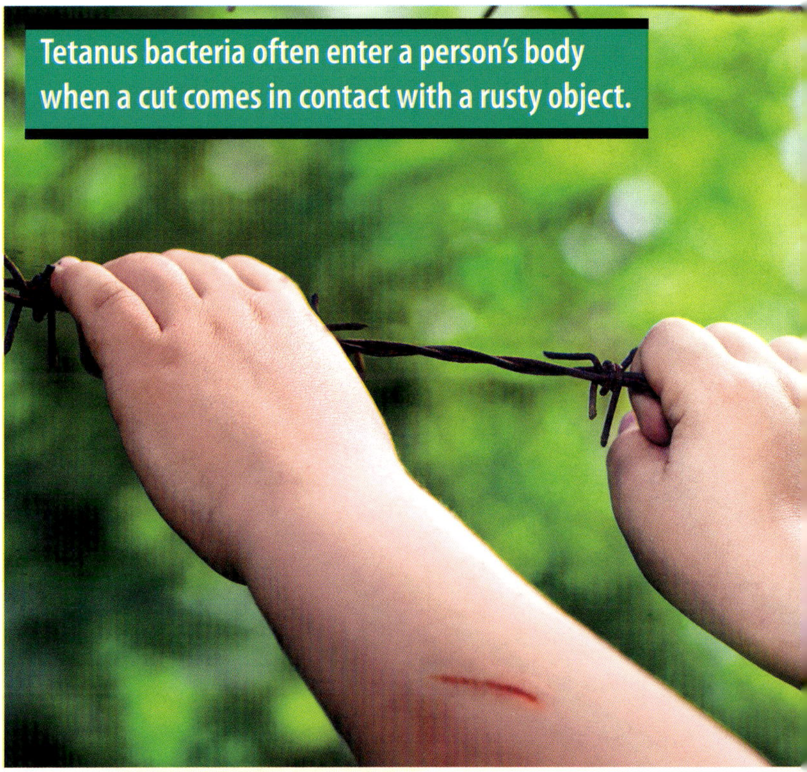
Tetanus bacteria often enter a person's body when a cut comes in contact with a rusty object.

PRO

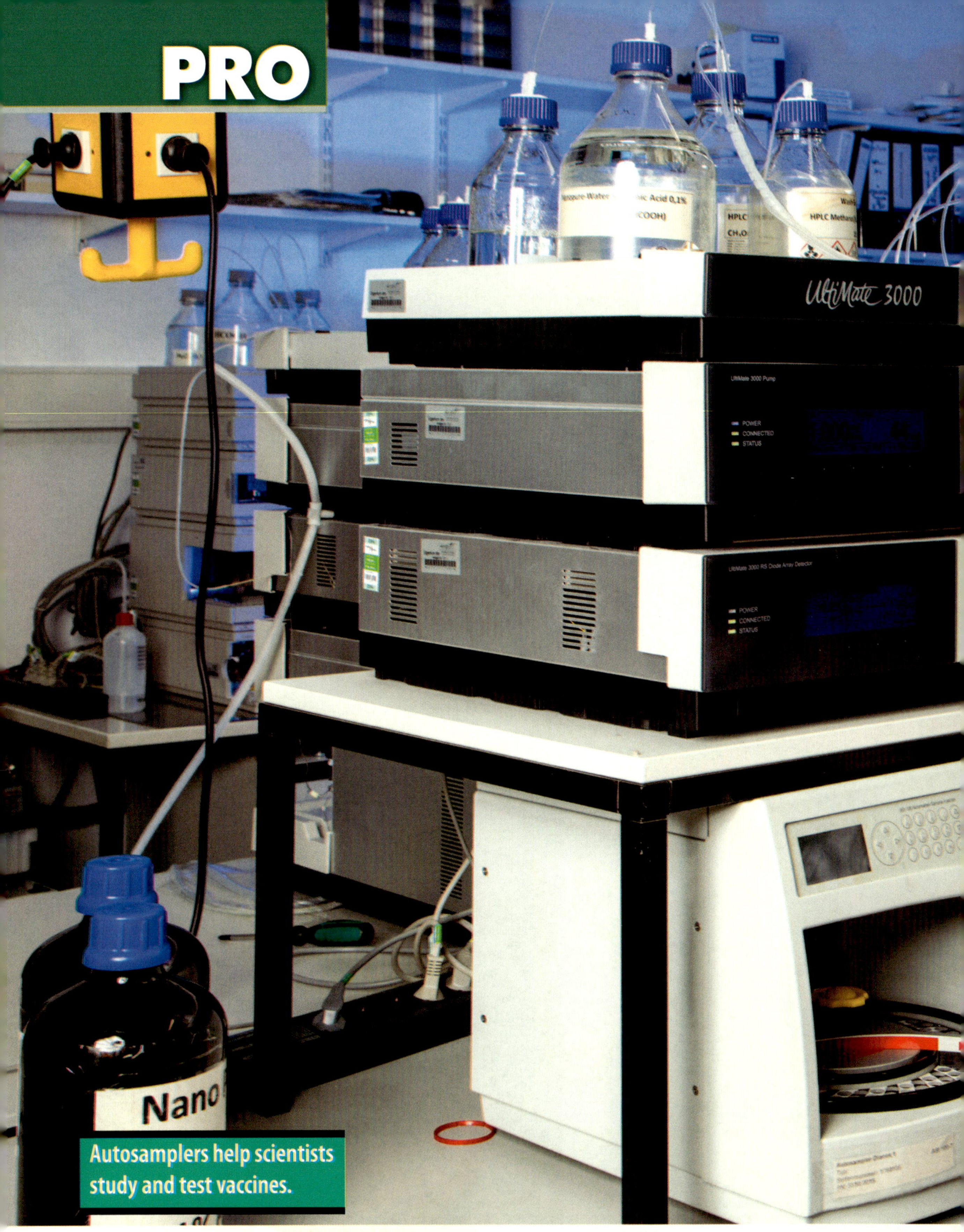

Autosamplers help scientists study and test vaccines.

Vaccines Are Safe and Cost-Effective

Trials test a vaccine's effectiveness.

In the United States, the Food and Drug Administration (FDA) monitors vaccines. This organization makes sure each vaccine goes through many tests before it is approved for worldwide use. First, scientists identify the antigens that could help prevent a disease. Then they test the vaccine on tissue samples and animals. They make sure it will be safe and effective.

Next, a manufacturer must get permission to make and test the vaccine. The manufacturer submits an application to the FDA. The FDA must approve or deny the application within 30 days.

After the FDA approves the application, the vaccine goes through three phases of testing. First, the vaccine is given to a small group of approximately 30 people. This test helps determine if the vaccine is safe. It also shows whether the vaccine provides immunity in humans. If the vaccine passes these tests, it goes on to the second phase. In this phase, hundreds of people receive the vaccine. The company also makes decisions about doses and schedules.

If these tests are successful, the vaccine moves to the third phase. This phase uses larger trials. They involve thousands of people. Researchers look for serious side effects that might not develop in the smaller trials. They also make sure the vaccine helps the body produce antibodies. If the large trials are successful, the vaccine developer applies to the FDA for a license. The FDA inspects the factory where the vaccine will be made. It also approves the labeling of the vaccine.

Each vaccine goes through many tests to make sure that it is safe.

The FDA is very selective. Only 46 new drugs were approved in 2017.

Even after a vaccine is licensed, the FDA keeps a close watch on its production. FDA employees inspect facilities. They study the manufacturer's tests of the vaccine. They may even conduct their own tests on the vaccine.

Public health officials also watch for side effects. If a side effect is linked to a vaccine, they weigh the benefits of the vaccine against the possible risks. They recommend whether the vaccine should be used.

It can take 10 to 15 years to develop and test a new vaccine. But preventing a disease is almost always less expensive than treating it. In 2016, a study showed that every dollar invested in vaccines saves $16 in health care costs. If fewer people get sick, less money will be spent on hospital stays and other medical expenses. In one year, for example, hospitals in Colorado treated 538 children for diseases that vaccines could have prevented. This cost $29.2 million, or more than $54,000 per child. A dose of a vaccine typically costs less than $200.

Many businesses offer their employees free flu shots.

PRO

Vaccines make it more difficult for diseases to spread.

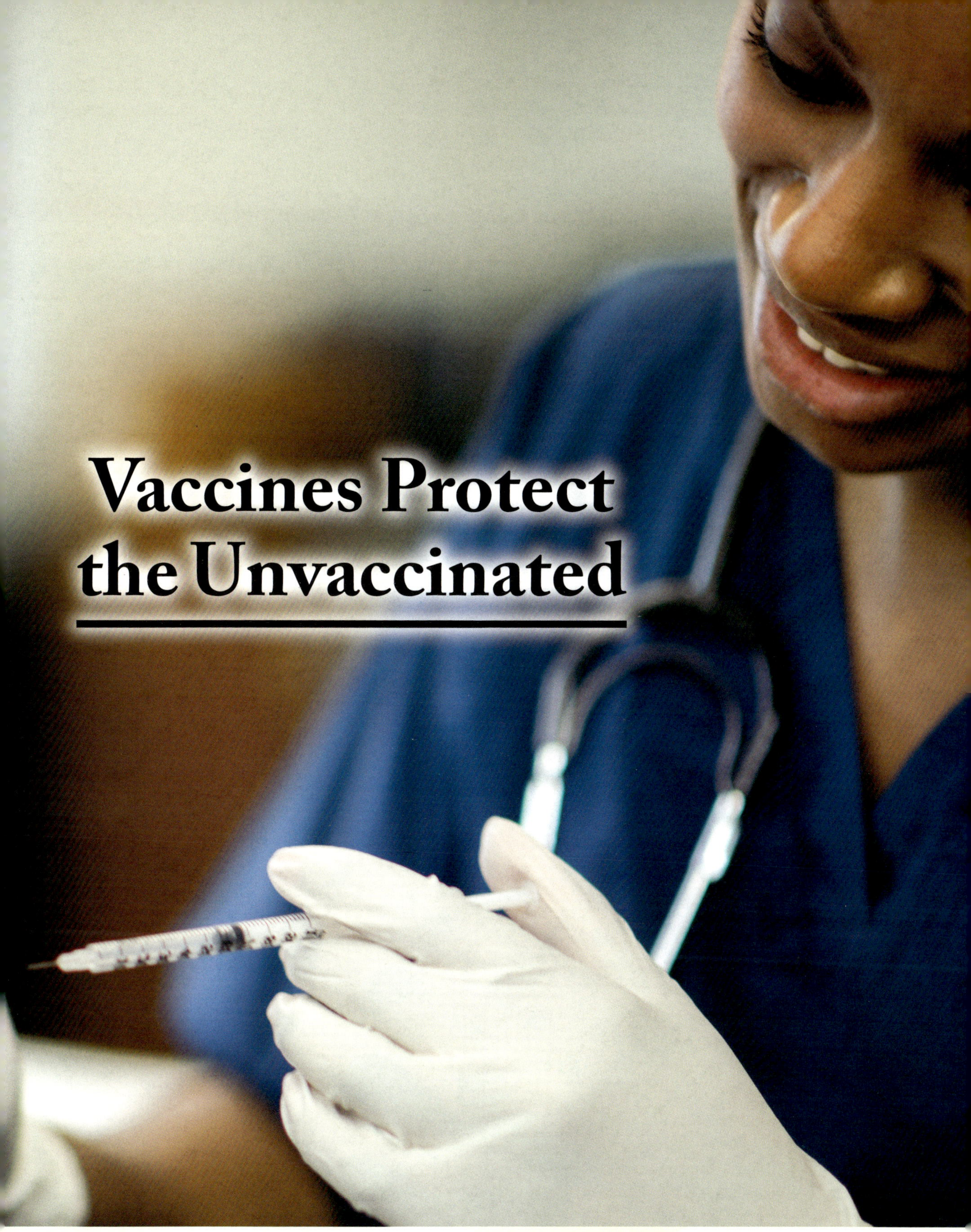

Vaccines Protect the Unvaccinated

Not everyone can receive vaccines. For example, babies who are less than one month old are too young to get them. People with serious illnesses such as cancer may not be able to receive vaccines either. But vaccines still help these people stay healthy. People who cannot receive vaccines rely on the immunity of others. If a person is immune to a disease, he or she cannot give it to someone else.

Immunization records keep track of which vaccines a person has received.

When more people are immune to a disease, it is harder for the disease to spread. This is known as herd immunity. But herd immunity breaks down when people who can receive vaccines do not. When fewer than 90 percent of children in a community are vaccinated, serious diseases can spread.

Approximately 3 percent of children in the United States are not vaccinated. But these children often live in the same communities. As a result, everyone in that community is at risk. Herd immunity will no longer prevent outbreaks of disease.

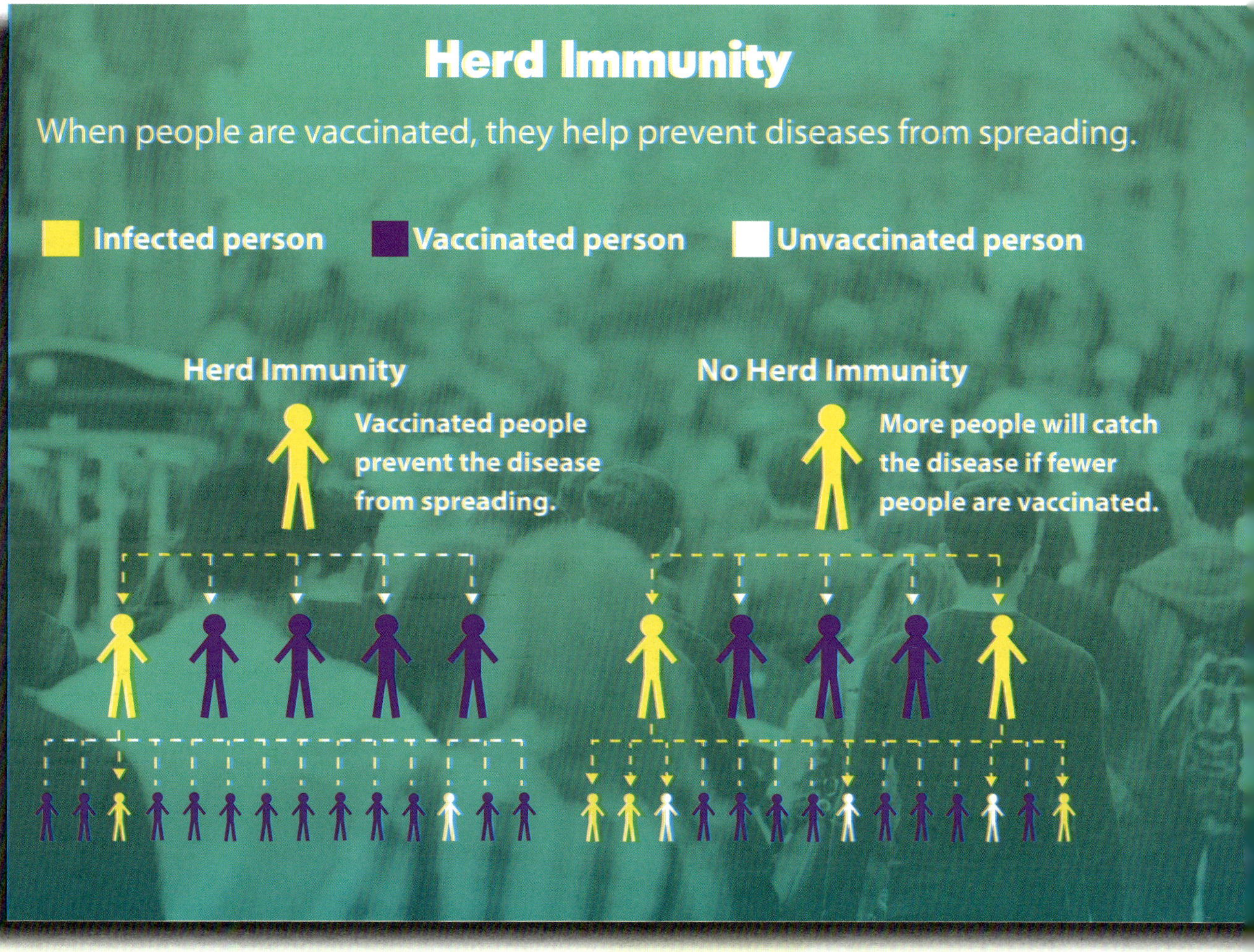

Some people think that if a disease is no longer occurring, vaccinations are not necessary. However, if vaccines are stopped, it can be easier for a disease to spread. Because people travel, diseases can spread rapidly. It takes only one traveler from another country where the disease is present to spark an outbreak. Polio, measles, and other preventable diseases could be spread throughout the world.

Vaccines and Autism

Autism is a disorder that makes it difficult to communicate with others. A study published in 1998 claimed that the MMR vaccine caused some children to develop autism. Later studies focused on thimerosal, a substance used in the MMR vaccine. Since 2003, however, numerous studies have shown no link between autism and the MMR vaccine. In addition, studies have shown no link between autism and thimerosal. The author of the original article even had his medical license revoked because of his dishonest study. Still, some parents choose not to vaccinate their children.

Outbreaks of serious diseases around the world have been increasing. For instance, the United States was free of measles in 2000. But some parents chose not to vaccinate their children. The herd immunity broke down. In 2011, 220 cases of measles were reported in the United States. The Centers for Disease Control (CDC) linked these cases to travelers returning from countries in Europe and Southeast Asia. In 2015, an outbreak of measles occurred at a large amusement park. The virus spread quickly. It took only a small group of people who were not vaccinated to fuel the outbreak. Many children got the disease. Vaccinations could have prevented many of these cases.

Many countries have mandatory vaccination programs. In France, 11 vaccines are mandatory.

CON

Not all vaccines guarantee lifelong immunity.

Vaccines Do Not Always Work

Organizations such as the Red Cross transport vaccines to many rural areas in developing countries.

Vaccines occasionally fail to prevent a disease. Sometimes, a person's immune system does not respond to a vaccine. Other times, vaccines fail because people make mistakes. Vaccines, especially live ones, must be handled correctly. Most need to be kept cool. Transporting the vaccine can take a long time. Some areas may not have cold storage to keep the vaccines alive. Then the vaccines do not work.

Errors can also happen when the vaccine is produced. For example, flu viruses change from season to season. It is difficult for people's immune systems to recognize the new viruses. Every year, scientists must try to match the antigens in the vaccine to the flu viruses being passed around the community. The vaccine for that year must protect against hundreds of flu viruses.

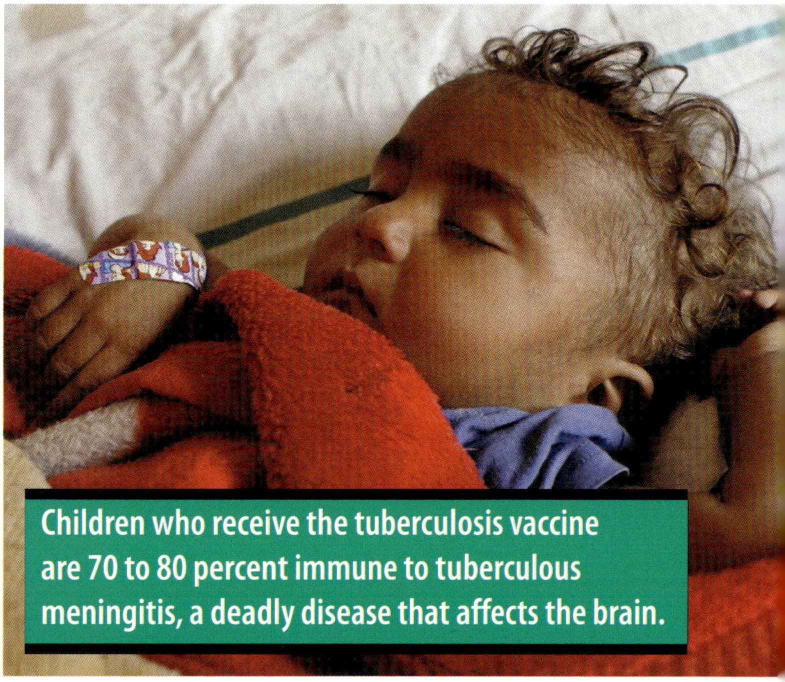

Children who receive the tuberculosis vaccine are 70 to 80 percent immune to tuberculous meningitis, a deadly disease that affects the brain.

Scientists must try to predict which virus will be most common. If the virus in the vaccine does not match the virus causing the infection, people will not be immune. Even when there is a good match, the vaccine only reduces the risk of flu by approximately 50 to 60 percent.

The Mutating Flu

Some flu viruses can live in animals. These viruses **mutate**. In some cases, they can cause sickness in humans. Scientists are constantly studying flu viruses. They pay close attention to viruses that begin where people and animals live close together. But staying one step ahead of the flu virus is very difficult.

Depending on how long the flu season lasts, a different flu virus can begin to circulate and make people sick. Developing a vaccine for this new virus can take months. It is also very expensive.

Other vaccines require multiple doses. Vaccines may be less effective when people do not complete the full number of doses. For example, the mumps vaccine requires several doses. If children receive one dose, they may be only 78 percent immune to the disease. Two doses of the vaccine will be approximately 88 percent effective. In some cases, even the full amount of doses may not completely protect a person from the disease.

Some vaccines cannot provide permanent immunity. People must receive booster doses. These additional doses expose the body to the antigens again. People must keep getting more doses to stay immune.

The tetanus vaccine lasts for approximately 10 years. After that, people must get a booster dose of the vaccine to stay immune. Other vaccines have shorter periods. For example, a typhoid vaccine must be given every two to five years.

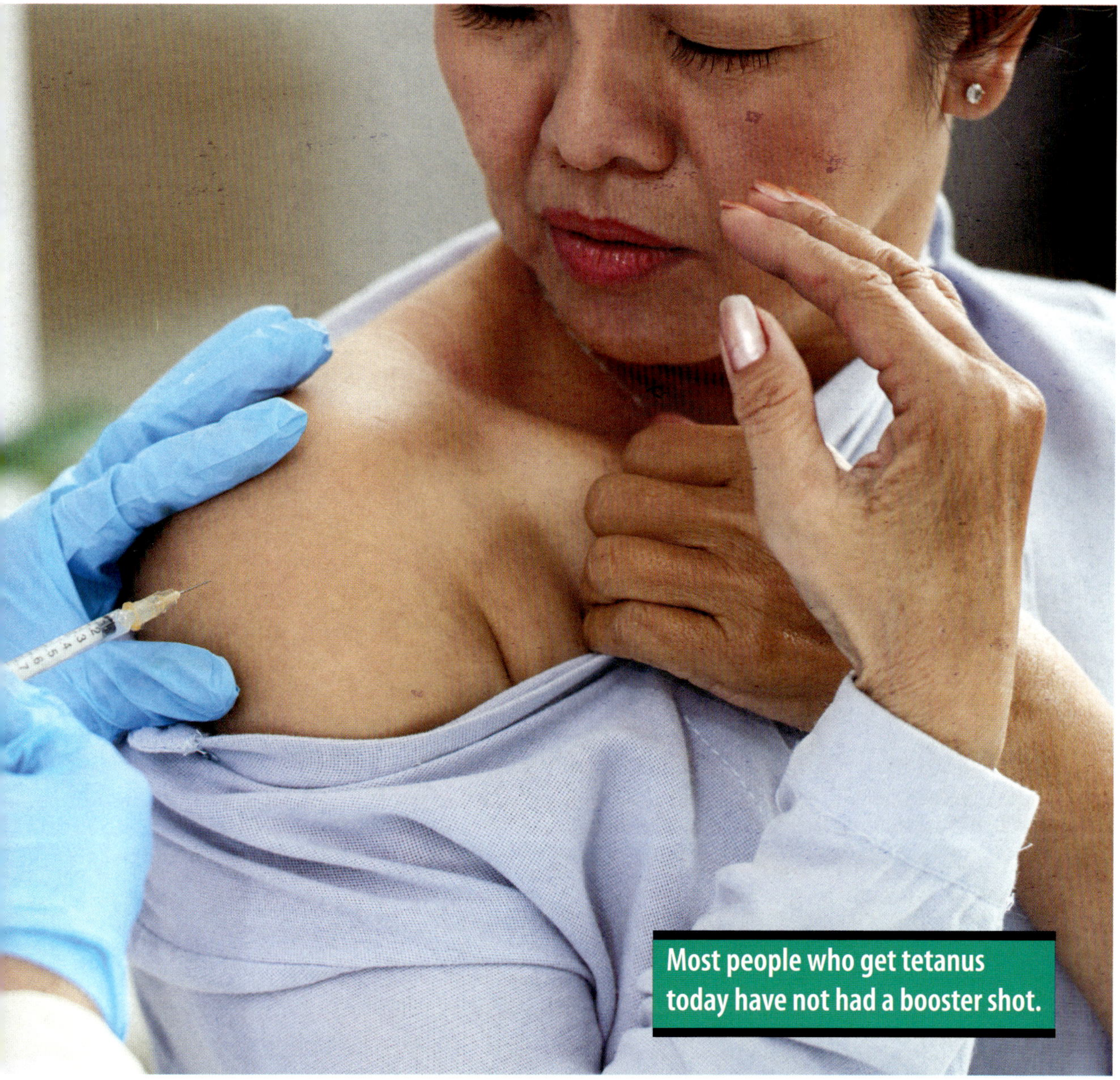

Most people who get tetanus today have not had a booster shot.

CON

People in South America, Central America, and Africa may be at risk of catching yellow fever, a disease carried by mosquitoes. However, some people are allergic to the yellow fever vaccine.

Not Everyone Should Be Vaccinated

A few vaccines contain ingredients that certain people are allergic to. For example, the yellow fever vaccine uses a virus that is grown in eggs. This vaccine contains a small amount of egg protein. People who are allergic to eggs could have a reaction to the vaccine. To avoid a reaction, they must go through a desensitization process. They must get several shots instead of only one. Each shot contains a small dose of the vaccine. An allergist gives the shots one at a time. The amount of vaccine in each shot is increased.

The MMR vaccine contains gelatin.

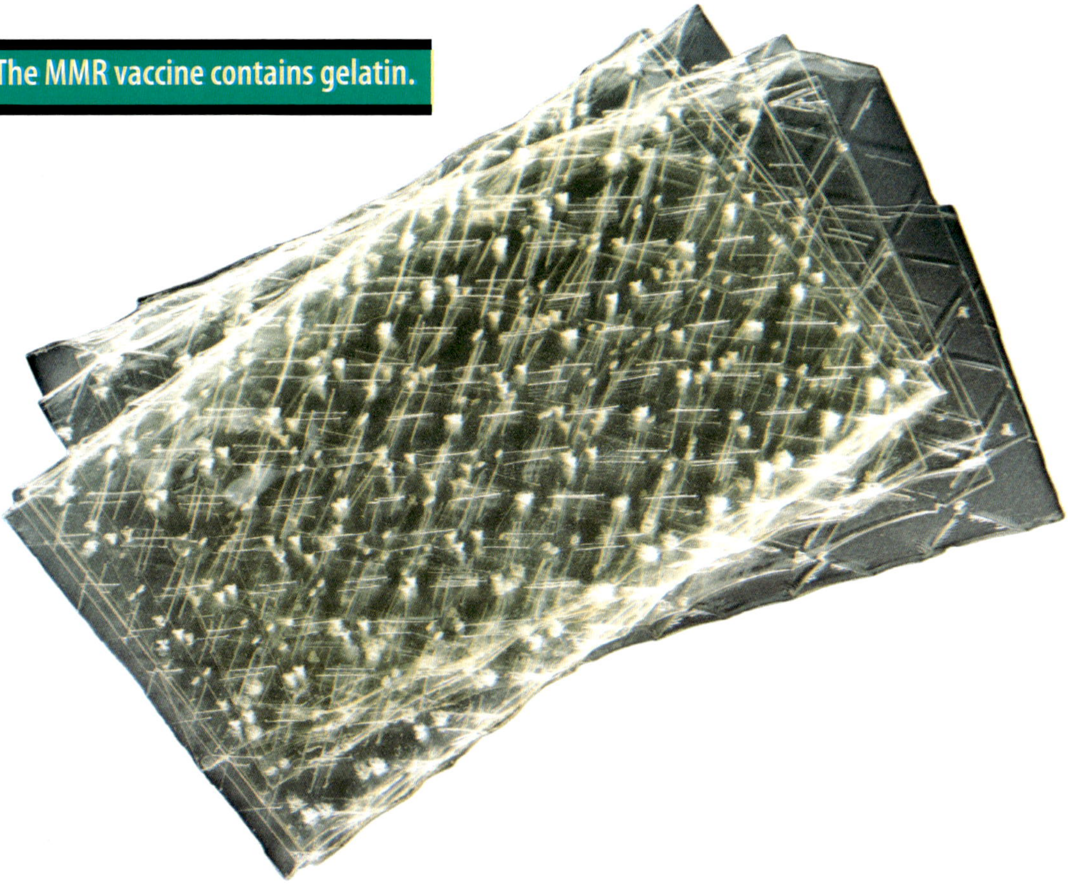

Gelatin can also cause people to have allergic reactions. The vaccines for chicken pox, yellow fever, and the flu use gelatin. Gelatin is the most common cause of an allergic reaction to a vaccine. However, reactions to gelatin are still rare.

People with damaged or weak immune systems are at risk, too. Vaccines might not work for them. These people's immune systems do not work properly. Cancer patients receiving radiation or medication often have damaged immune systems. So do people with human immunodeficiency virus (HIV), heart disease, and other chronic illnesses.

Did You Know?

Approximately one in one million children has a life-threatening allergic reaction to vaccines. Signs of a severe allergic reaction include hives and difficulty breathing.

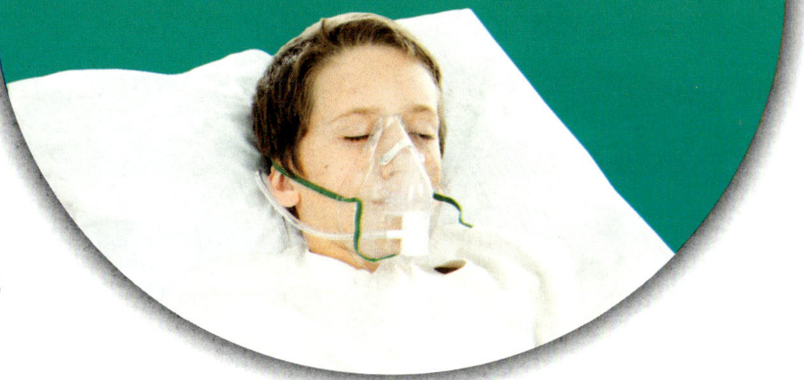

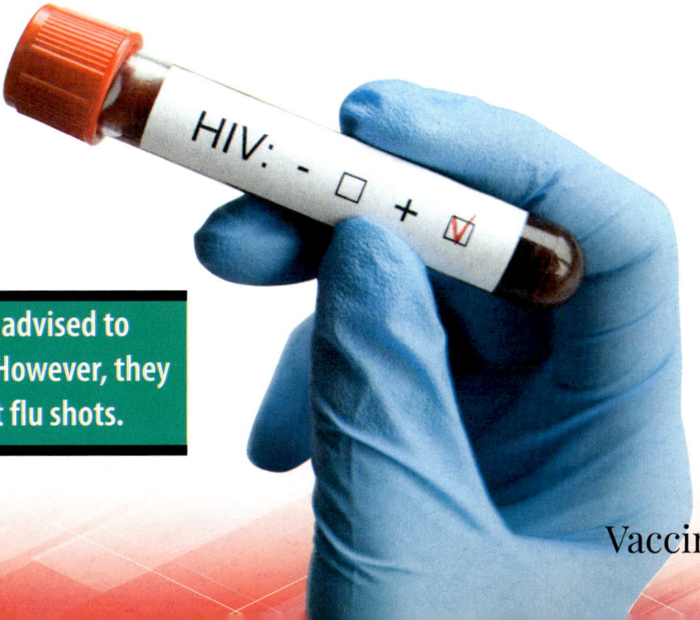

People with HIV are advised to avoid live vaccines. However, they can safely take most flu shots.

Organ transplant patients should avoid contact with people who have recently received the smallpox vaccine.

Organ transplant patients are given large doses of medicine to reduce their immunity. This helps prevent their bodies from rejecting the new organs. However, it also weakens their immune systems.

People with weak immune systems are often warned not to receive vaccinations. Often, their bodies will not produce immunity to the disease. In some cases, the vaccine may even harm them. Their bodies may not be able to fight the viruses in some vaccines.

Live vaccines pose the biggest threat to people with weak immune systems. Measles, polio, and chicken pox vaccines usually contain live viruses. Live viruses are used to make nasal mist flu vaccines. People with weak immune systems cannot fight off the live germs in these vaccines. They may develop an infection. The vaccines may make them sick.

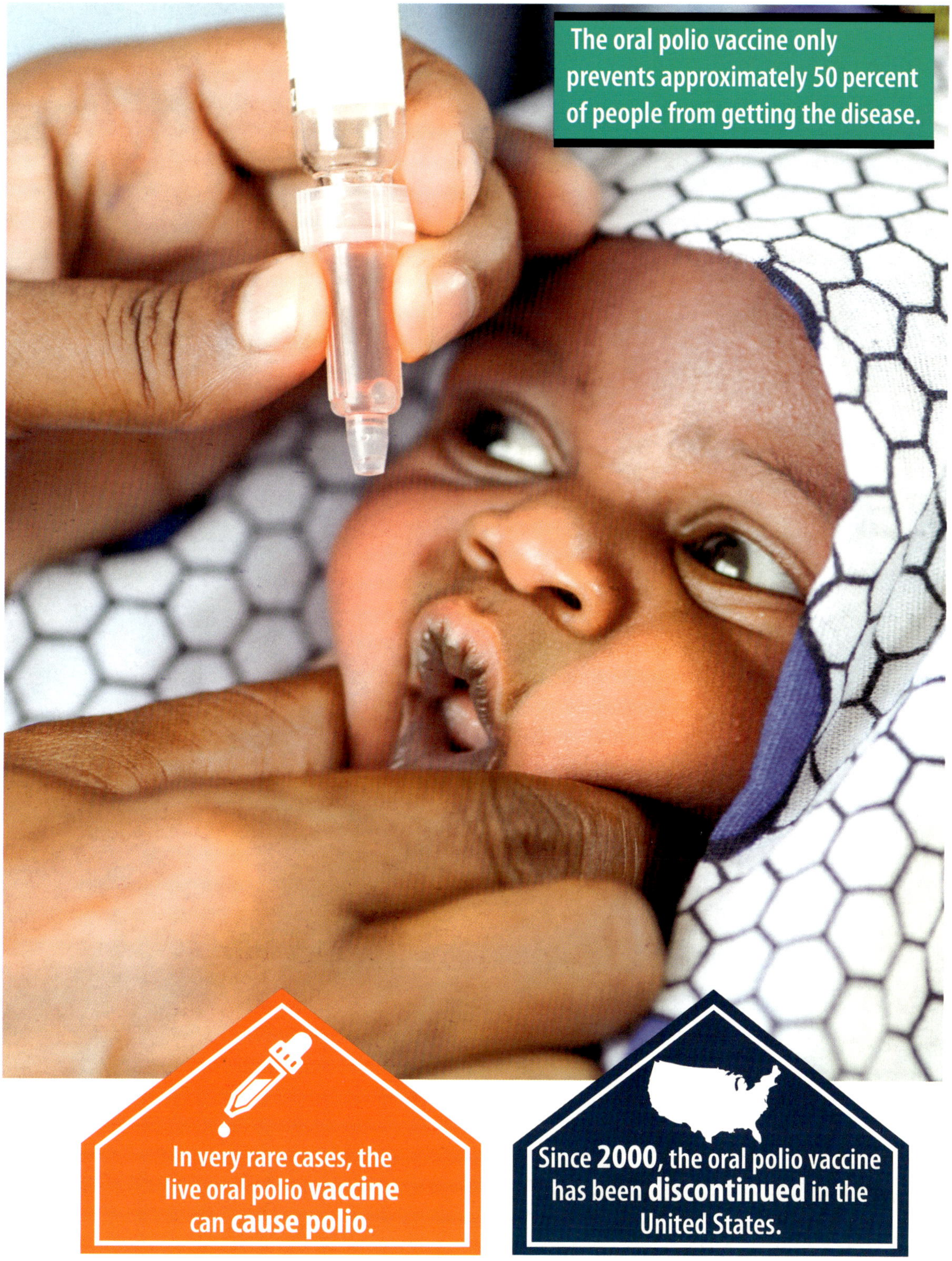

The oral polio vaccine only prevents approximately 50 percent of people from getting the disease.

In very rare cases, the live oral polio **vaccine** can **cause polio.**

Since **2000**, the oral polio vaccine has been **discontinued** in the United States.

CON

Some children develop redness and swelling where the shot was given.

Vaccines Can Cause Side Effects

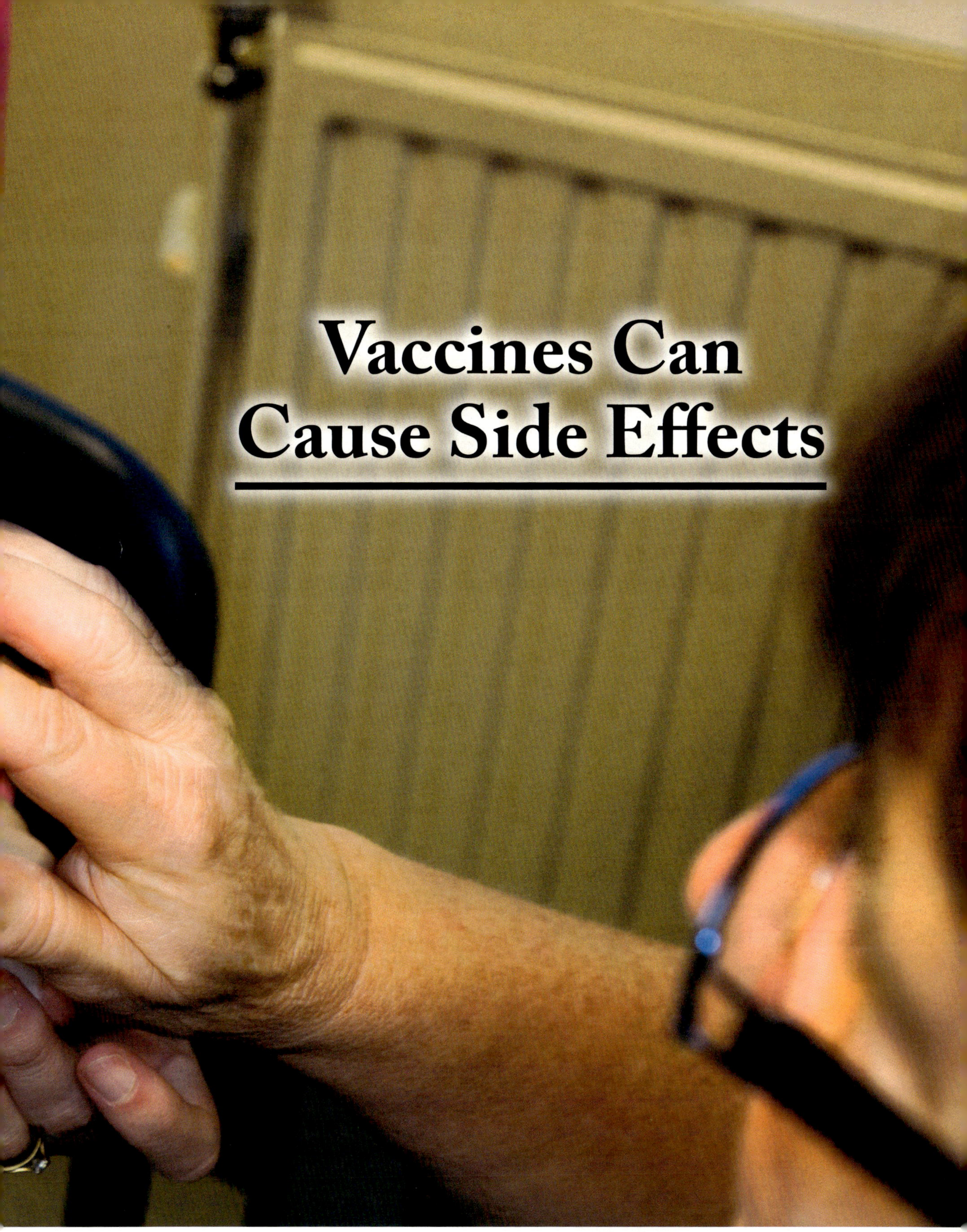

The chicken pox virus causes a rash of painful blisters.

Some vaccines have side effects. These side effects are not nearly as serious as the diseases that the vaccines prevent. But they are still unpleasant. For example, vaccines for chicken pox and measles can cause a mild fever or rash. But these reactions usually do not last long.

Although it is rare, vaccines can have more serious side effects. A few people have had difficulty breathing after receiving vaccines. Others had rapid heartbeats or chest pain. Some felt dizzy or faint. People have also reported nausea, vomiting, or diarrhea after receiving a vaccine.

In a few cases, side effects are severe. For example, the MMR vaccine causes **seizures** in approximately one in 3,000 doses. In extremely rare cases, some people have suffered deafness or permanent brain damage after the MMR vaccine.

According to some sources, the chicken pox vaccine may cause seizures or other severe reactions. A few children have developed pneumonia after getting this vaccine.

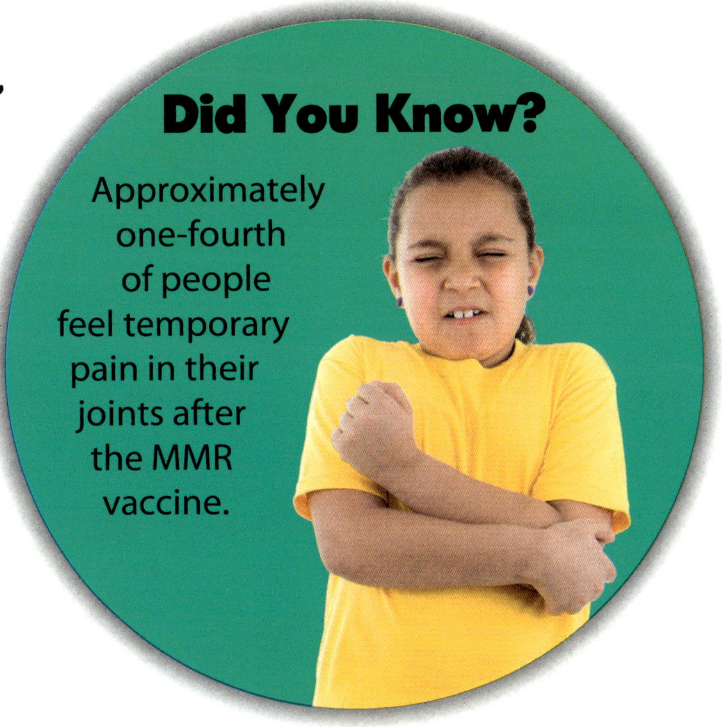

Plus, the chicken pox vaccine uses a live virus. Family members can be exposed to the disease when a child is vaccinated. Adults and teenagers may develop serious complications if they get chicken pox.

In 1990, the United States created the Vaccine **Adverse** Event Reporting System. Since then, approximately 30,000 cases of harmful reactions to vaccines have been reported each year. Approximately 85 to 90 percent of these reactions are mild. But 10 to 15 percent are serious. This means the vaccines have caused permanent disability, life-threatening illness, or death.

A few people have died after receiving a vaccine, though this is very uncommon. In 1994, approximately 160 people died after getting a tetanus shot. That same year, approximately 140 people died after getting a polio vaccine. But these numbers vary from year to year. Other years, fewer than 100 people died after getting the vaccine for tetanus or polio.

The flu and pneumonia vaccines have the most risk of causing death. More than 100 people in the United States die each year after receiving these vaccines. But that is still a very small percentage of the millions of people who get these vaccines.

It is important to weigh the benefits of vaccines against the possible side effects. Some people are at greater risk for side effects than others. Before getting a vaccine, each person should talk with his or her doctor.

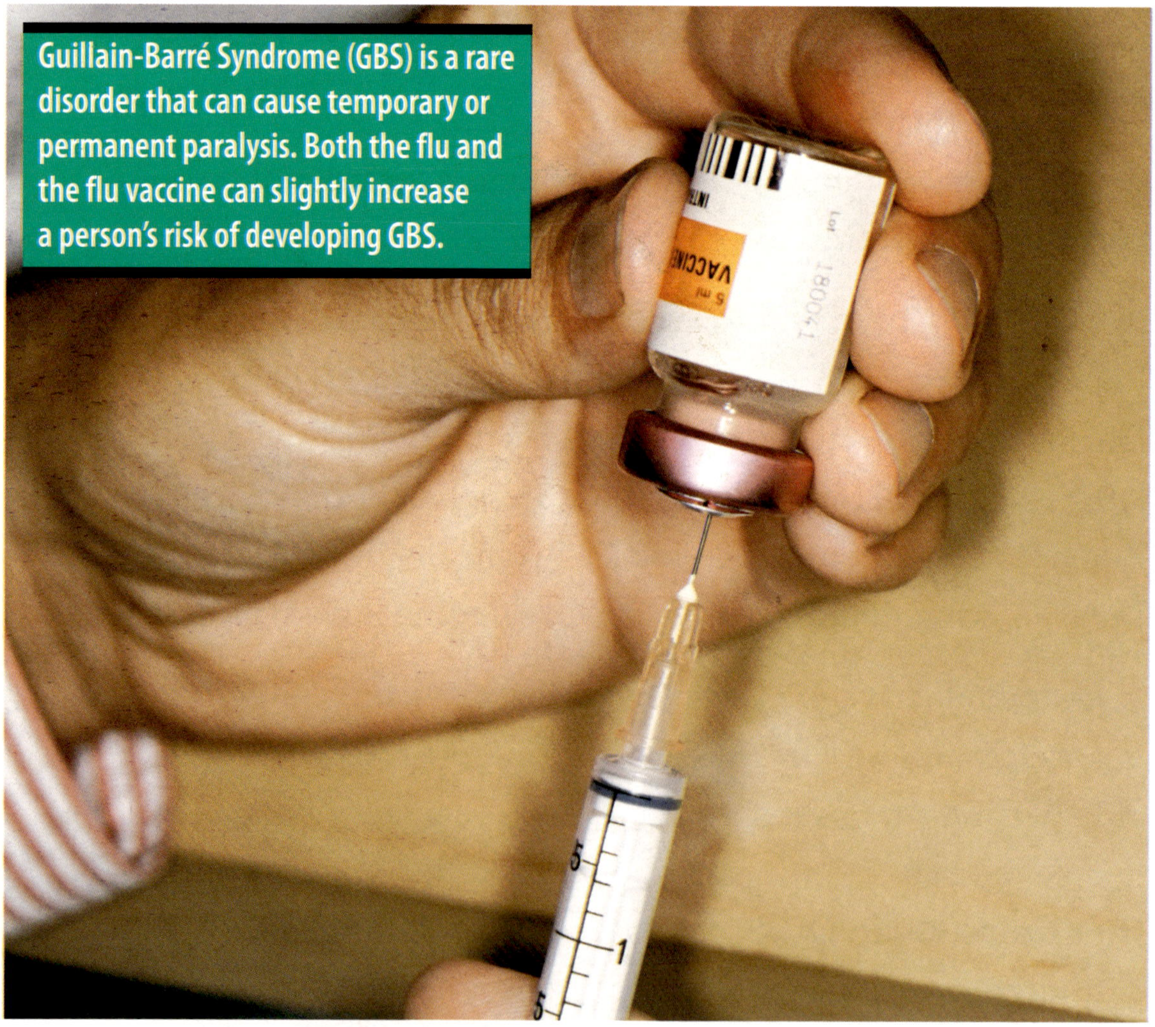

Guillain-Barré Syndrome (GBS) is a rare disorder that can cause temporary or permanent paralysis. Both the flu and the flu vaccine can slightly increase a person's risk of developing GBS.

Pros and Cons Summary

PROS

- Vaccines protect people from dangerous diseases and complications.
- Vaccines have reduced the number of deaths caused by illnesses.
- The FDA's system of testing and trials ensures that vaccines are developed and manufactured safely.
- Vaccinating against a disease is less expensive than treating it.
- Vaccines have greatly reduced outbreaks of serious diseases worldwide.
- Herd immunity even protects people who cannot get vaccines.

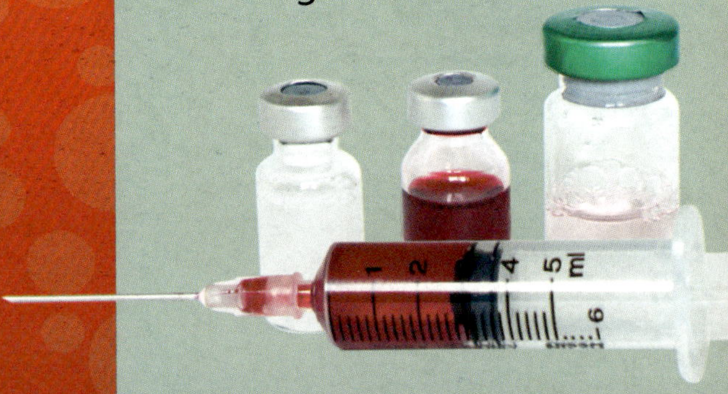

CONS

- Errors in vaccine production or storage can lead to vaccines that do not work.
- People must receive multiple doses of some vaccines to produce immunity.
- A few people are allergic to ingredients that are used to make vaccines.
- Some people are not able to receive vaccines.
- Vaccines can have unpleasant side effects.
- In extremely rare cases, side effects from vaccines can be serious or even life-threatening.

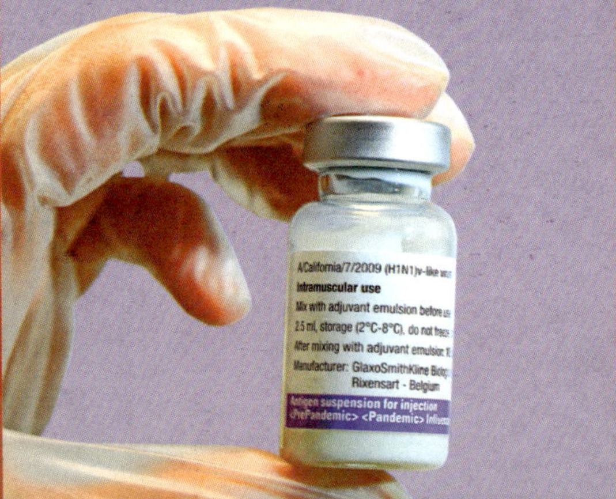

Vaccines Map

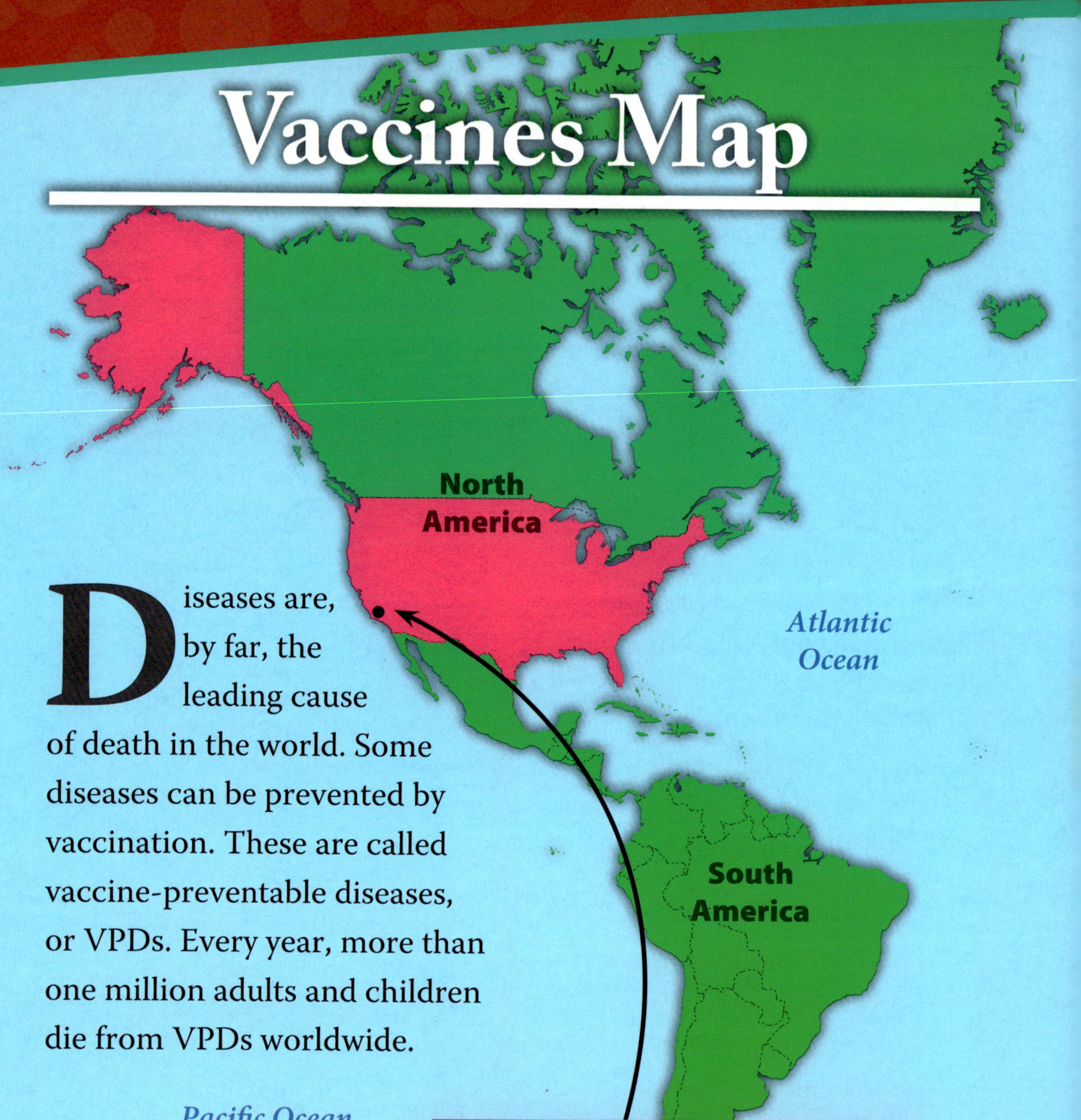

Diseases are, by far, the leading cause of death in the world. Some diseases can be prevented by vaccination. These are called vaccine-preventable diseases, or VPDs. Every year, more than one million adults and children die from VPDs worldwide.

United States In December 2014, an outbreak of measles began in California's Disneyland Park. By February 2015, about 125 people were infected. Most of them had not been vaccinated against measles.

Switzerland In 2012, the World Health Organization, headquartered in Geneva, began implementing its Global Vaccine Action Plan. The plan aims to provide universal access to vaccines, with the goal of preventing millions of deaths by 2020.

India In 2017, a leprosy vaccine developed by the National Institute of Immunology, New Delhi, was piloted. Human trials began in the Indian states of Gujarat and Bihar, where there are thousands of new leprosy cases each year.

Guinea In 2013, a two-year-old boy died of the Ebola virus in the village of Meliandou. He is believed to be the first victim of an Ebola outbreak that killed an estimated 11,325 people by the end of March 2016. Since then, an effective Ebola vaccine has been developed, although it is not yet licensed.

Quiz

1
Which three kinds of white blood cells does the body use to fight germs?

2
How many people died because of smallpox in the 20th century?

3
What are some diseases that have been mostly eradicated in the United States because of vaccines?

4
Which U.S. federal agency is responsible for monitoring vaccines?

5
Can vaccines protect unvaccinated people from a disease? Why or why not?

6
In order to stay immune from tetanus, how often do people need a booster dose of the vaccine?

7
Which substance is the most common cause of allergic reactions to vaccines?

8
Which U.S. program collects reports of harmful reactions to vaccines?

ANSWERS **1.** Macrophages, B-lymphocytes, and T-lymphocytes **2.** Nearly 300 million **3.** Measles, tetanus, and polio **4.** Food and Drug Administration (FDA) **5.** Yes, because of herd immunity **6.** Every 10 years **7.** Gelatin **8.** Vaccine Adverse Event Reporting System

Key Words

adverse: creating harmful results

antibodies: proteins that fight infections by attaching themselves to antigens and destroying them

antigens: proteins that disease-causing organisms use to attach themselves to cells in the infected body

complications: medical problems that arise in addition to the main disease being treated

immune system: the body system that uses specialized cells to fight infections

membranes: thin layers of tissue that cover some parts inside the body

mutate: to develop a new trait as a result of changes to genes

nervous system: the body system that picks up and sends nerve impulses to other parts of the body

paralyzed: unable to move a part of the body

pneumonia: the infection of one or both lungs

seizures: extreme twitching of muscles because of unusual brain activity

World Health Organization: an international organization that works to improve public health worldwide

Index

Log on to www.av2books.com

AV² by Weigl brings you media enhanced books that support active learning. Go to www.av2books.com, and enter the special code found on page 2 of this book. You will gain access to enriched and enhanced content that supplements and complements this book. Content includes video, audio, weblinks, quizzes, a slide show, and activities.

AV² Online Navigation

AV² was built to bridge the gap between print and digital. We encourage you to tell us what you like and what you want to see in the future.

Sign up to be an AV² Ambassador at www.av2books.com/ambassador.

Due to the dynamic nature of the Internet, some of the URLs and activities provided as part of AV² by Weigl may have changed or ceased to exist. AV² by Weigl accepts no responsibility for any such changes. All media enhanced books are regularly monitored to update addresses and sites in a timely manner. Contact AV² by Weigl at 1-866-649-3445 or av2books@weigl.com with any questions, comments, or feedback.